ANIMAL BEHAVIOR

Animal
Courtship

ANIMAL BEHAVIOR

ANIMAL BEHAVIOR

Animal
Courtship

KRISTA WEST

CHELSEA HOUSE
PUBLISHERS
An imprint of Infobase Publishing

Chelsea House
An imprint of Infobase Publishing
132 West 31st Street
New York NY 10001

Library of Congress Cataloging-in-Publication Data

West, Krista.
  Animal courtship / Krista West.
     p. cm. — (Animal behavior)
  Includes bibliographical references and index.
  ISBN 978-1-60413-090-4 (hardcover)
  1. Courtship in animals. I. Title. II. Series.
  QL761.W43 2009
  591.56'2—dc22   2008040121

Chelsea House books are available at special discounts when purchased in bulk quantities for businesses, associations, institutions, or sales promotions. Please call our Special Sales Department in New York at (212) 967-8800 or (800) 322-8755.

You can find Chelsea House on the World Wide Web at
http://www.chelseahouse.com

Text design by Kerry Casey
Cover design by Ben Peterson and Alicia Post
Printed in the United States
Bang EJB 10 9 8 7 6 5 4 3 2 1
This book is printed on acid-free paper.

All links and Web addresses were checked and verified to be correct at the time of publication. Because of the dynamic nature of the Web, some addresses and links may have changed since publication and may no longer be valid.

Cover: A pair of king penguins playfully interact.

Contents

Human Courtship

> If she do frown, 'tis not in hate of you,
> But rather to beget more love in you:
> If she do chide, 'tis not to have you gone;
> For whay, the fools are mad if left alone.
> Take no repulse, whatever she doth say;
> For—get you gone—she doth not mean—away.
>
> —William Shakespeare (1564–1616),
> *The Two Gentlemen of Verona*

ENGLISH POET AND PLAYWRIGHT William Shakespeare (1564-1616) often wrote about the complicated relationships between love-struck men and women. In this quote, from the play *The Two Gentlemen of Verona*, Shakespeare describes a woman that acts harshly toward a man, but is romantically interested in him at the same time. He wrote the play nearly 500 years ago.

Today, **courtship** between two humans is no less complicated. Courtship occurs when one person attempts to win the love and affection of another. It often results in two mature members of a species becoming a couple, and many sexually mature animals practice courtship with the intent to mate and produce offspring (children).

In the animal world, species of insects, birds, fish, shellfish, reptiles, amphibians, and mammals each have their own sets of courtship rules and rituals. Some species dance to attract a mate. Some glow. Others talk or sing. Some attack and fight. Humans may flirt or act disinterested.

Human courtship is complicated by human culture. Shakespeare, perhaps as much as anyone, seemed to understand these two basic parts. There is a biological side of human courtship—the desire to produce healthy offspring—that affects everything that dating humans do. But there is also a cultural side of human courtship—the desire for love and romance—that affects the process as well.

THE BIOLOGY OF HUMAN COURTSHIP

The human courtship process is rooted in human biology. The biological goal of human courtship is to create a mating pair that can produce healthy offspring. Yet, two humans must first meet and agree to form a mating pair. In much of the modern world, this process is known as dating.

Many of the tactics used by dating humans to attract other individuals are rooted in our biological history. As University of California San Diego biologist Helen Fisher describes in *Psychology Today's* "The Biology of Attraction," many modern courtship tactics—including the standard date ingredients such as flirting, making eye contact, dancing, and eating—are fairly predictable parts of the biological courtship process.

Flirting

Traditionally, flirting is the first step of human courtship. Flirting involves different actions that are used to attract attention. As it turns out, humans are pre-programmed to flirt.

Flirting is usually the first step of human courtship. The act was particularly innocent and playful during the Victorian era (mid-to-late 1800s), as portrayed in this image.

Sociologists—scientists interested in the behavior of humans—spend hours watching men and women court each other in public places. They have found that the flirting process for men and women is fairly standard. A woman might smile at a man, lift her eyebrows, and open her eyes wide. Then she quickly tilts and drops her head, breaking her gaze. Frequently, says Fisher, "she also covers her face with her hands, giggling nervously as she retreats behind her palms." These brief periods of contact convey a woman's interest while protecting her at the same time.

Likewise, men have a predictable set of flirting behaviors. A man might respond to a woman by arching his back and thrusting out his chest in an effort to show strength and dominance.

Many male animals attempt to look big, strong, and "puff up" when flirting. Codfish stick out their heads and fins. Snakes, frogs, and toads inflate their bodies. Antelope, deer, and chameleons turn sideways to show their big bodies. Cats arch their backs and bristle their fur. Lobsters open their claws and stand tall. Gorillas pound their chests. Human men, it seems, attempt to look big and strong during courtship as well.

Making Eye Contact

Eye contact between two interested humans has a powerful, immediate impact during the courtship process. A person often cannot ignore another human looking directly at him or her. Eye contact demands a reaction. A person can return the look (inviting contact) or look away (expressing disinterest).

The process of making eye contact is also predictable. "Men and women often stare intently at potential mates for about two to three seconds," says Fisher, "during which their pupils may dilate—a sign of extreme interest."

Many suggest that the power of eye contact to initiate the courtship process is one reason that some human cultures require

LOVE AT FIRST SIGHT SCIENCE

Can a man and woman really fall in love at first sight? Romeo and Juliet did. Science suggests that love at first sight is possible.

Animals often select mates quickly so that a healthy match is not lost to another individual. For example, the squirrel-mating season is short. A female squirrel needs to mate quickly. If she sees a healthy male squirrel that is willing to mate, she gains nothing by wasting time. To produce healthy offspring, it is in the female's best interest to mate with the desirable male quickly, before the chance is lost.

Some scientists suggest that perhaps humans might also select healthy mates quickly, before the chance slips away. Even if science doesn't support the idea, many humans say they have experienced love at first sight.

women to wear veils and prevent eye contact between men and women.

Dancing Together

According to anthropologist David Givens and biologist Timothy Perper, as reported in a *Psychology Today* article entitled, "The Biology of Attraction," the human courtship dance has a few basic steps. First, courting humans establish a territory. A man or woman chooses a seat, leans against a table, or takes a spot at the bar. This is the "territory" in which he or she feels comfortable.

Next, the man or woman moves in ways that attract the attention of other humans. A man may stretch or swagger when he walks. A woman may twist her hair or arch her back. These movements attract attention and give people something to do with their nervous energy.

If two individuals are interested in one another, the final step happens when the pair begins to move in the same ways. A couple may turn their chairs or move to face each other until their shoulders are aligned. Then they begin to move in tandem. When he crosses his legs, she crosses hers. First she leans left, and then he does. "Dancing" together is another part of human courtship.

Feeding the Mate

If a man takes a woman out for dinner and pays the bill, the woman is often being courted. The dinner date is a common courtship ritual for humans. It is common for men around the world to give women food and gifts in hope of attracting a mate.

Human males aren't the only ones offering food to females. These courtship feedings likely have an important biological function. They show that the male is a good provider or hunter, and worthy of being a mate. In humans, dinner and a gift might tell a woman that the man has the money and resources to care for her and her offspring. This is a reminder that the biological goal of human courtship is still a part of the process.

THE CULTURE OF HUMAN COURTSHIP

In general, human culture teaches people what to value. Some cultures value the dating process. Other cultures skip dating altogether.

The Western culture tends to value the romance and love that are ideally discovered during courtship. For many people, the goal of human courtship is not to have children, but to fall in love.

Modern human courtship is likely quite different from the courtship process between early humans. As British scientist W.P. Pycraft first wrote in his book *The Courtship of Animals* in 1914 (republished in 2007), in order to understand modern human courtship, "We must get back, so far as is possible, to the very dawn of the human race: to that period of man's evolution when his conduct was controlled by purely savage instincts."

These "purely savage instincts" meant that early humans formed couples quickly, in order to mate and have children. They probably did not fall in love. Yet, as human culture developed,

COMPUTERIZED COURTSHIP

Humans have long used culture-based matchmaking tools to meet potential mates. They have written love letters, gone on blind dates, talked to fortunetellers, and placed or answered newspaper personals. Meeting and talking via computer is the latest cultural matchmaking tool.

Online dating allows people to find and meet others online, and to get to know them through e-mail or instant messaging. An online dater might use an online dating service to post personal information. The person might include a photo, likes and dislikes, hobbies, his or her age, as well as whether or not he or she smokes, has children or wants children, and more.

That person is then able to electronically search the Web and find the personal information of other individuals. The purpose is to help users find potential matches quickly using his or her personal search criteria. If the online dater finds someone interesting, he or she would likely send an introductory e-mail. Ultimately, if the over-

(continues)

(continued)

the-computer conversations go well, a more traditional, face-to-face meeting might be arranged.

Online dating has become a serious and widespread way for men and women to meet, according to the non-profit Pew Internet & American Life Project (PIALP), an organization dedicated to exploring the impact of the internet on society. The PIALP's 2006 report, *Online Dating*, found that:

- About 63 million people—31% of American adults—said they know someone who has used a dating Web site.
- About 53 million people—26% of American adults—said they know someone who has gone on a date with a person they met through a dating Web site.
- About 30 million people—15% of American adults—said they know someone who has been in a long-term relationship or who has married someone who was met online.

Online dating was once considered a matchmaking tool for a small number of people. Now, millions of people use online dating services to find potential mates. The biological goals of courtship are still part of the process, but the human computer culture is a significant part as well.

human courtship developed as well. Soon, love became a part of the process.

Some suggest that romantic love first became a requirement for human courtship sometime in the Middle Ages in Europe (between the fifth and fifteenth centuries). Or, at least, this is when people first started to write about and record tales of human love.

During this time, the idea of courtly love became widespread. Courtly love is a combination of physical desire and a deeply emotional desire for another person. People thought that experiencing courtly love could make them nobler, stronger, and happier. British knights King Arthur and Sir Lancelot often felt empowered by romantic love for Queen Guinevere.

Yet, with the powerful force of courtly love came strict rules to keep this force under control. Cultures developed courtship rules. In many non-Western cultures, **arranged marriages** became common. Parents or families set up a marriage based on practical factors, such as social class and income. They hoped that romantic love would develop once the couple got together. Arranged marriages are still common in some parts of the world and among some religions today.

In many North American and European cultures, by contrast, each person is responsible for finding his or her own mate, or choosing not to find one at all. In these cultures, finding someone who strongly appeals to the human senses—with the potential for love—is a major part of the courtship process.

THE EVOLUTION OF COURTSHIP

The human courtship process—like the courtship processes of other animals—is not an accident. Human and animal courtship rituals are the result of **evolution**. Evolution is the process of passing on characteristics and behaviors from generation to generation. Over hundred, thousands, and even millions of years, evolution is the driving force that shapes courtship in the animal world.

2

The Natural History
of Courtship

ANIMAL COURTSHIP IS one small part of the **natural history**—or study of plants and animals in their natural environments—of life on Earth. By studying a plant or animal's natural history, scientists can help understand it. Natural history helps explain various traits, such as why animals eat what they eat, why they look the way they look, and why they act the way they act. Together, the actions and appearances resulting from an animal's natural history work as a set of tools. Some of these tools are used during the courtship process.

The tools of animal courtship fall into two basic categories: **physical characteristics** and **behaviors**. A physical characteristic is something that can be seen on an animal's body, such as a color or an appendage (for example, a feather or a fin). A behavior is a response of an organism to signals or individuals in its environment, such as a song or a movement.

These physical characteristics and behaviors are the products of natural history. They have evolved over time because they helped animals survive and reproduce. One behavior may help an animal find food, or a certain physical characteristic may help an animal defend itself from other animals.

Charles Darwin's theory of natural selection helped explain how physical and behavioral advantages helped animals survive and therefore reproduce and pass on their specific traits.

One of the first people to document these tools of natural history was British scientist Charles Darwin (1809-1882). Before Darwin, there was no scientific reason for why a peacock maintains its huge, colorful feathers. Darwin is famous for helping to explain the physical characteristics and behaviors observed in the natural world, including things that happen during animal courtship. Most of his scientific ideas and explanations still stand true today.

THE THEORY OF NATURAL SELECTION

Charles Darwin is famous for posing many new theories about natural history. A **theory** is a set of ideas used to describe some aspect of the world. Theories can be repeatedly tested until they are widely accepted as fact. This is the case with gravitational theory, for example. Each theory starts out as a hypothesis: a testable idea. The idea that there is life on other planets is not a hypothesis because it cannot be tested at this time. No one can survey every planet in every corner of space.

Darwin's theory of **natural selection**, first described in his 1859 book *The Origin of the Species*, is now widely accepted. Natural selection is the process by which favorable characteristics and behaviors are passed down from generation to generation, gradually spreading through a population over time.

Each organism has certain physical characteristics (Darwin called them "traits") that help or hurt its chances of surviving and mating. In winter, when food is scarce, a moose with longer legs may have a better chance of finding food high on trees, so that moose will have a greater chance of living through the winter. A moose that can survive a long winter and still be healthy and strong will have a better chance of successful courtship and mating in the spring. It will pass on some of its long-legged genes to its offspring.

Darwin's Research

Darwin first came up with his ideas of natural selection by looking at the world around him. The son of a successful country doctor, the 22-year-old Darwin sailed around the world for five years on a 90-foot ship called the *HMS Beagle*. The voyage began in December 1831. His thoughts and writings from this trip eventually became one of the most influential books of all time: *The Origin of Species.*

When Darwin joined the expedition, he considered himself an amateur scientist. However, he was recruited for the voyage largely because the captain, Robert Fitzroy, wanted someone to keep him company.

After years sailing up and down the western coast of South America, mapping the edges of the continent, the sailors spent five weeks exploring the Galapagos Islands. It was in this land of giant tortoises and diverse birds that Darwin first began to develop his idea of natural selection.

Darwin noticed that many of the animals living in the Galapagos Islands looked a lot like the animals living on mainland South America, but they were not exactly the same. Further, there were small differences between animals living on the different islands within the Galapagos. Each island tortoise, for example, had its own distinct shell design. The shells were similar, but unique to each small island.

From these observations, Darwin concluded that animals from South America had colonized the Galapagos Islands, and that each population of animals had changed slightly over time to survive in each new environment. The idea that different but similar animals existed was not ground breaking. However, Darwin was the first person to suggest a **mechanism**, or series of steps, for how these animals were created.

Darwin called this mechanism natural selection (also called the "survival of the fittest"). The theory of natural selection includes the idea that animals with physical or behavioral advantages are most likely to survive and reproduce into the next generation, passing along their advantageous traits to their offspring.

Over time, these advantageous traits change a population of animals so that it looks or acts differently than before. Eventually, a population may change so much that it becomes a new species.

During Darwin's time, no one understood exactly how such traits were passed from generation to generation. Most people believed that God created and designed all life and all animals, and that new animals did not evolve naturally (some people still believe this is the case; they are called creationists.)

When Darwin first published his theory of natural selection in *The Origin of Species* in 1859, he used his observations from the *HMS Beagle* voyage to support his ideas. He became the first British scientist to argue that God is not solely responsible for creating new animals. The claim was not an easy one for him to make.

DARWIN'S DILEMMA: THEN AND NOW

After Darwin's travels to the Galapagos, he spent a few years living in London. Then, he married his first cousin, Emma. They moved to a house in the country, where Darwin raised 10 children, wrote, and did research. During this time, his thoughts on natural selection as a mechanism for evolution took shape, as did his dilemma.

Darwin waited nearly a quarter of a century after his *HMS Beagle* voyages to fully publish his thoughts on evolution. Darwin, it seems, had a personal, moral dilemma. To say that species were not spontaneously created by God, but evolved slowly from other species—through courtship and reproduction—went against much of what he and his family believed.

Charles and Emma Darwin were very religious people. When Charles returned from his voyage, Emma was concerned that his ideas on evolution would send him to hell in the afterlife. She was tormented by the fact that they might spend eternity apart. Darwin, likewise, was uncomfortable with his own thoughts.

As early as 1844, Darwin wrote to a friend that to publish his thoughts on evolution would be akin to "confessing a murder." Today, the apparent conflict between religion and science continues.

Modern-day, literal readers of the Bible believe that God created the Earth and all of life in six days—an idea known as creationism. *The Origin of Species* explains how the creation of life on Earth took place over millions of years—the theory of evolution.

Present-day creationists argue that evolution is unproven. Most scientists say that the evidence for evolution is clear. Recently, some people have combined creationism and evolution in a concept known as **intelligent design**.

Intelligent design contends that evolution cannot be the only force that shapes life on Earth because life is so clever that it must have an intelligent designer. This idea says that evolution does happen, but it is only possible with God's influence. There is no science to prove intelligent design, but it continues to prompt debate among creationists and evolutionists.

The November 2005 issue of *Natural History Magazine* was devoted to Charles Darwin. In that issue, scientist and science writer Richard Dawkins writes about natural selection: "People have a hard time believing that so simple a mechanism could deliver such powerful results." Yet, he argues, the mechanism of natural selection has resulted in life forms that look deliberately designed.

Perhaps Darwin had a hard time believing in the power of natural selection as well. In the last years of his life, Darwin suffered from mysterious stomach and heart troubles. Some experts said he might have picked up a parasite while traveling in South America. Others believe Darwin was anxious about where his thoughts on evolution might lead him and the rest of the world.

Legend has it that on his deathbed, Darwin confessed his sinful thoughts on evolution and repented, but his family always

THE DIVERSITY OF LIFE

Over many generations, natural selection results in the widespread **diversity** of life. Diversity is a measure of how many different types of things exist.

Big cities are diverse because they have people with many different nationalities and cultures. Life on Earth is diverse because there are many varieties of plants and animals. The more varieties there are, the greater the diversity. Many scientists estimate there are between 2 million and 100 million species of animals on the planet.

Ecologist Edward O. Wilson is known worldwide for his research and writings about the diversity of life. According to Wilson, 1 gram of soil from a beech forest holds as many as 5,000 species of bacteria. A paper clip weighs about 1 gram, as does a U.S. dime.

Wilson says such diversity should be valued as a work of art. In his book, *The Diversity of Life*, he writes, "Each species is a masterpiece, a creation assembled with extreme care and genius." Such diversity relies on successful courtship to produce generations and generations of offspring.

has denied such claims. Darwin died in 1882 and was entombed with honor at Westminster Abbey.

SEXUAL SELECTION

Natural selection explained much of what Darwin observed during his trip through South America and the Galapagos Islands. Yet, it could not explain everything. Why, Darwin wondered, did some creatures maintain elaborate or cumbersome traits without clear functions? The answer, Darwin reasoned, has its roots in animal courtship.

Peacock feathers are the classic example of a costly trait that can't be explained by natural selection alone. The feathers are costly because they require a lot of energy to grow (just as healthy hair for humans requires a good diet). They are also large

Darwin's theory of sexual selection explains that while a peacock's feathers give the bird no clear survival advantage, their attractiveness to potential mates is the reason they continue to be passed on genetically.

and heavy. This makes it difficult for peacocks to move around and to hide from potential dangers.

According to Darwin's theory of natural selection, traits are passed on from generation to generation only if they give each animal some advantage. Yet, peacock feathers, at first glance, appear to offer only disadvantages. To explain the development of peacock feathers (and other similar animal features), Darwin developed the theory of **sexual selection**.

The theory of sexual selection says that traits that increase an animal's success during courtship and mating are favored from generation to generation. Behaviors or appearances that make one animal attractive to the opposite sex during courtship ultimately are passed on to offspring. Peacock feathers, according to Darwin's theory, are the result of sexual selection.

Today, scientists understand that many of the physical differences between males and females are the result of sexual selection. At the same time, sexual selection is the driving force behind the courtship behaviors of many animals.

Physical Characteristics

A physical characteristic is an observable body part, such as a color or an appendage (for example, a feather or a fin). Darwin realized that sexual selection allows animals to develop specialized physical characteristics for two main reasons: to fight and to show off.

Some male animals develop specialized physical characteristics to help them compete for access to mate with females. Horns, antlers, and body size can give one male an advantage over another during battle for a female.

Body size is one of the most common examples of a physical characteristic that results from sexual selection. In many animals, the male is larger than the female. Male elephant seals, for example, can be 18 feet (5.5 m) long and weigh 5,000 pounds

These elephant seals lined up on the beach at Sea Lion Island in the Falkland Islands illustrate the size difference between males and females. A male (*left*) lies with a female (*middle*) and a younger sea lion.

(2,270 kg). Females are about 10 feet (3 m) long and weigh 1,430 pounds (650 kg). The larger size of the males is attributed to sexual selection. The larger a male elephant seal is, the better he can fight off other males for a chance to mate.

Males may have physical characteristics that allow them to show off for females. Vivid colors and patterns, elaborate feathers, or other physical frills help males to appeal to potential mates.

The male green anole lizard, for example, has a bright red, bubble-like flap of skin under its throat. When courting a female anole, the male inflates its red throat while bobbing its head up and down. Both the red color and the eye-catching inflatable

A male anole can extend a reddish flap of skin, called a dewlap, on its neck. The dewlap is prominent when the male is trying to attract a female or defend territory.

bubble are the products of sexual selection, helping make the male more attractive to a female.

Physical characteristics that can be altered by sexual selection are known as secondary sex characteristics. In many animals, the males display most of these secondary sex characteristics.

Behaviors

A behavior is the response of an organism to its environment. During animal courtship, males and females use behaviors such as dancing, vocalizing, and gesturing to make themselves more

WHY BOYS HAVE ALL THE FUN

In most cases of sexual selection, the males possess the unusual secondary sex characteristics. The male gets the bright yellow feathers. The male gets big, beautiful antlers. The male gets the throbbing red throat bubble. The male dances a dance or sings a song. Lest females be jealous, there is a clear reason why the boys have all the "fun."

The male and the female play different roles in the final goal of animal courtship: reproduction. They both work to pass on their traits to healthy offspring, but each has costs associated with conceiving and rearing young.

In most animals, the male's job is to fertilize the female. The male's investment of time and energy happens quickly. After mating, males do not typically invest much time in developing or taking care of offspring. As a result, males use their energy to try to fertilize as many females as possible. The more females that a male fertilizes, the more offspring he will have.

In contrast, the female lays eggs (and often takes care of them) or carries the offspring as they develop, in addition to helping them survive after birth. A female's investment of time and energy lasts longer. It is in her best interest to mate with a healthy, strong male. His genes are more likely to help produce healthy, strong offspring. Because the female invests more time and energy in her offspring, she wants them to have the best chances possible of surviving to reproduce.

These basic rules of biology govern the world of sexual selection. A female is often particular about the male she chooses as a mate. So males often compete with other males for the chance to mate with the females. The secondary sex characteristics develop because of this competition. Successful males pass their secondary sex characteristics to their male offspring. And the fun begins again.

attractive to potential mates. Through sexual selection, these behaviors are passed on from generation to generation.

To get the attention of females, the male frigate bird combines unusual physical characteristics with a mating dance and a

A male frigate bird entices females to mate by inflating its gulgar sac—a large throat bag. When a female flies overhead, the male will move its head side-to-side and shake its wings while calling out to the female. If she's interested, she'll land beside the male.

mating call. These large black birds can take 20 minutes to inflate their bright red throats like balloons. They then wait for females to fly overhead. When a male sees a female, he wags his head from side to side, shakes his wings, and calls. If the dance is successful, the flying female will land and mate with the male.

NATURAL REACTIONS

The frigate bird, like many other birds, uses calls and songs to attract females. Many other animals use behaviors to attract mates. Spiders dance. Frogs croak and sing. Some monkeys use color to stand out. The rituals of animal courtship are diverse and detailed, and not yet entirely understood. Scientists still have much to learn.

3

Insect and Arachnid Courtship

TOGETHER, INSECTS AND ARACHNIDS are the most common and most diverse group of animals on the planet. They can all be found in a large group of animals called the **arthropods**.

Insects are small invertebrate animals with three pairs of legs, one or two pairs of wings, and three main body sections. Insects include beetles, butterflies, flies, and ants.

Arachnids have a body in two segments, four pairs of legs, and no antennae or wings. Examples of them include spiders, ticks, and scorpions. By some estimates, arthropods account for more than 9 out of every 10 animals on Earth. The population alone is very large and diverse. Scientists say there are more different kinds of arthropods on Earth than all other types of animals combined. These creatures live in many places and have many different courtship rituals.

Insects and arachnids often use physical tools—including movements, gestures, touch, and even light—during courtship. Many spiders, for example, dance and jump during courtship. Butterflies flit and float in the air. Fireflies light up. Other insects and arachnids touch tails or antennae to communicate during courtship. Each of these physical signals works to help them recognize others of their kind, or species.

BEETLE COURTSHIP

A **beetle** is an insect with a rigid wing. About 40% of all insects are beetles, and new species are discovered almost every day. Beetles live everywhere on Earth except in the oceans and the

Mating between two dung beetles may occur within a ball of dung.

polar regions. During courtship, they often use physical aggression, scent, and light.

Some types of male dung beetles have horns on their heads. They use the horns to fight with other males for a female's attention. Other dung beetle varieties have antennae that help them "sniff out" potential mates.

Dung beetles feed on the dung, or solid wastes, of other animals. During courtship, the male and female often mate underground or inside a ball of dung. The female lays eggs in the dung. When the eggs hatch, they have a food source waiting. Dung

ROLE REVERSAL IN WATER BUGS

In insect and arachnid courtship, it is often the female that calls the shots. She chooses her mate, when to mate, and how long mating lasts. The males must often tread carefully. Many present females with gifts of food; sometimes the male himself is the meal. Many different types of female spiders, for example, often eat the male after mating—including the Redback, Black Widow, Golden Orb, and Crab spiders.

Yet, things are different in the courtship of the Zeus water bug, a resident of Australia's eastern coast. Female water bugs provide niceties for the males during courtship.

The male Zeus water bug measures only about half the size of the female. During courtship, he rides on the female's back eating a gift of protein-rich wax that she secretes from an organ near her head. The male will eat and mate with the female for as long as a week.

Scientists suspect that it's easier and takes less energy for the female to carry the male than it does to look for a new male each time she is ready to mate. Together, they ensure offspring for the next generation.

beetles are common in the United States. They are often used to control solid waste on cattle farms.

A different type of beetle uses light to attract a mate during courtship: the firefly, or lightning bug. Adult male fireflies spend every evening of their lives flashing their lights to attract females. A male will fly a few feet above the ground and flash its light in a specific pattern. The females sit on the ground. A female responds to a male with a single flash. The male lands, finds the female, and mating begins.

Males seeking mates must be careful though—female fireflies of some species will trick unsuspecting males. These tricky females will match the light patterns of other species, drawing males looking for mates. Yet, instead of mating, the females will eat the males.

BUTTERFLY AND MOTH COURTSHIP

Butterflies and moths are closely related insects known for their unusual life cycles. They start life as caterpillars. Then, they enclose themselves in cocoons (moths) or chrysalises (butterflies). After weeks or even months, they emerge as winged insects. Butterflies and moths use their wings to dance while courting potential mates.

Each species of butterfly and moth has its own dance pattern. In general, the male will fly above or behind the female while fluttering his wings to attract attention. If the female is interested, she lands. The two may touch antennae or rub their legs together before mating.

Male butterflies of many varieties will place a physical barrier on the female after mating. Known as a **mating plug**, the barrier prevents other males from mating with the female. Some butterfly mating plugs are made of greasy substances spread on the female. Others are cap-like structures that are put in place after mating.

Many male insects use mating plugs to keep females from mating with other males, but the method is particularly common in butterflies.

COCKROACH COURTSHIP

Cockroaches are common insects that live in many environments on Earth. They are often considered city pests, but only a small number of cockroach varieties live in cities. Most cockroaches live in rural areas and tropical places. During courtship, female cockroaches typically use gestures and scent. Males use gestures and songs.

A female cockroach often begins the courtship process by stretching her lower body and raising her wings. She then sends out a chemical signal called a **pheromone** from her back. If a male picks up the signal, he approaches her. Typically, the male and female will touch antennae in a sword-like fight before mating.

Some varieties of cockroaches, including the hissing cockroach of Madagascar, will also "sing" during courtship. Males produce a loud hiss that can be heard by humans up to 12 feet (3.7 meters) away. The males hiss when fighting with other males for a female, when courting a female, and during mating.

SCORPION COURTSHIP

Scorpions are distinct-looking arachnids. They have very poor eyesight and can only see about an inch in front of them. Yet, they have a very sensitive sense of touch. A scorpion's body is covered with tiny hairs, which the scorpion uses as feelers. Not surprisingly, the sense of touch is the most important tool used during scorpion courtship.

Female Madagascar hissing cockroaches are attracted by loud male hisses during courtship.

On the undersides of a scorpion's body are specialized organs used for touch called **pectines**. Pectines look different in male and female scorpions, and scientists suspect scorpions use pectines to help distinguish between males and females of their own kind during courtship.

Scorpions raise and link their tales together during courtship, which leads to a courtship dance.

When two scorpions are courting, they approach each other face-to-face. Then they raise and intertwine their tails. (Although the tails can sting humans and other animals, scorpions are immune to the stings.) The male will often pull the female along in a sort of dance, which can last many hours in some varieties of scorpion, until the two find a place to mate.

After courtship and mating is complete, the female scorpion sometimes eats the male. This happens among many other arachnids, too. Scientists suspect much of the courtship dance is the male's way of telling the female that he is not just a piece of food. He wants to mate first.

SPIDER COURTSHIP

Both male and female spiders have special courtship tools. Female spiders dominate courtship in size and behavior, but male spiders have their own set of physical tools and gestures.

Females usually control the courtship and mating process of spiders, and display strong **sexual dimorphism**. Sexual dimorphism occurs when males and females of the same type of animal are different sizes or colors, or have different body parts. The female spiders are often much larger than the males, and most do not hesitate to eat the males. Some female spiders, such as the Australian redback spider, are known for devouring males immediately after (or even during) mating.

INSECT ILLUSTRATOR: ARTHUR SMITH

Not everyone who is fascinated by insects becomes a scientist. Arthur Smith (1916-1991) made a career of drawing insects at the Natural History Museum of London. During his lifetime, Smith created nearly 20,000 accurate, detailed line drawings of insects. Many of his illustrations appear in scientific books and field guides.

Smith became interested in natural history as a young boy in England. At age 15, he went to art school. He began working at the museum in 1940. He worked on his illustrations side by side with insect experts, to ensure the accuracy of his work. Smith developed a technique using ink, watercolors, and pencil.

In one of his well-known illustrations from 1960, Smith shows the dramatic courtship behavior of the common British spider (also called the hunting spider). The illustration

(continues)

(continued)

shows the smaller, male spider presenting the larger female with a meal as a mating gift: a fly wrapped in a web. If the female accepts the gift, the male will wait until the female's fangs are safely embedded in the meal. Then he will mate with her while she eats. This illustration is displayed in the public galleries at the Natural History Museum.

Smith is most famous for drawing insects, but he also drew other animals, rocks, and landscape scenes.

Perhaps as a result of this female dominance, male spiders have developed a diverse set of skills. In some species of spiders, the male will simply run to the female and mate with her. Yet, in most species, the process is more complicated.

In many species, a male spider will pluck or dance on a female's web. This lets the female know that he is a courting male, rather than just a juicy meal. In other species, a male entertains a female while they mate. A male crab spider will wrap the female in silk while they mate. The male European nursery web spider presents a dead fly to the female for a meal to eat while mating. In still other species, the male holds the jaws of the female open with his legs to keep from being eaten during mating.

A male spider uses a special set of arm-like appendages called **pedipalps** during courtship. They hold sperm and transfer it into the female during mating. If mating occurs more than once, the male refills his pedipalps with sperm.

TOUGH LOVE

Insect and arachnid courtship, it seems, isn't always easy. It's a physical challenge for some. Plus, because many of them are natural predators, males risk being eaten by their mates immediately following courtship. This, in part, is what makes insect and arachnid courtship an interesting topic to study.

4

Fish and Shellfish Courtship

FISH AND SHELLFISH include many animals that are classified in different groups. Most fish with bones and fins are considered one group. *Shellfish* is a non-scientific term that includes many edible animals without bones, such as clams and crabs. There is quite a bit of variety among these animals. Both goldfish and sharks are fish, but they are very different. Sea urchins, crabs, and squid all are considered shellfish.

In many cases, fish and shellfish mating occurs outside the animals' bodies. They release eggs and sperm into the water, and fertilization happens by chance. Because of this, many fish and shellfish do not choose mating partners, and courtship is not important. But there are exceptions.

Many species of fish with courtship rituals do so with the aid of color and movement. Salmon, for example, turn bright red during courtship. Other fish use bright colors to attract potential mates near nests, where eggs and sperm are more likely to meet.

Shellfish courtship is more complicated. Shellfish with heads, arms, or legs will use movements and gestures when courting. Male lobsters gently stroke females prior to mating. Shellfish without heads or limbs, such as oysters and sea urchins, have very few courtship rituals, if any. Some do use chemical signals to let potential mates know that they are ready to reproduce.

THE FISH AND SHELLFISH POPULATION

More than 70% of Earth's surface is covered with water. Therefore, it's not surprising that there are a lot of fish and shellfish on the planet.

Fish make up more than half of all **vertebrate** species on Earth. Scientists have found fossil fish that lived 400 million years ago. Fish have been around for a long time.

Fertilization happens outside the body for echinoderms, such as the sea urchin.

Fish are found in many environments. They live in obvious places, such as oceans and lakes. Fish also live in high mountain streams, desert springs, cave ponds, and deep ocean trenches. Scientists group almost all fish with fins and bones in a group called the **actinopterygians**. There are about 24,000 species of actinopterygians on Earth.

Shellfish include many groups of animals. **Crustaceans** include animals with shell-like outer skins, such as crabs and lobsters. **Bivalves** are animals with two-part shells, such as clams and oysters. Some **cephalopods** have inner shells; these include octopuses and squids. **Echinoderms** are a group of animals with spiny or rigid skins. Sea stars and sea urchins are echinoderms.

There are about 30,000 varieties of crustaceans, 15,000 different kinds of bivalves, 700 varieties of cephalopods, and about 7,000 different types of echinoderms. Some bivalves and crustaceans live in fresh water, but most other shellfish live in the salty waters of oceans.

FISH COURTSHIP

Fish courtship is a little different than the courtship of many other animals. Fish can mate without touching each other. A female fish deposits a package of eggs underwater. A male fish swims over the eggs and fertilizes them.

The courtship that leads up to this mating depends on the type of fish, but it often involves color and movement. Fish may change color during courtship. This shows that they are ready to mate. Then, the male and female may "dance" before mating. Salmon are known for their color changes, while sticklebacks are known for their mating dance.

Salmon is a name for several varieties of fish. Before they mate, salmon leave the oceans where they live their adult lives

A male stickleback fish builds a nest, which will be used as a place to fertilize a female's eggs.

and travel inland to the same freshwater streams in which they were born.

As the salmon travel upstream, they slowly change color. They go from silvery-blue to vibrant reds and pinks. Once upstream, the females will deposit packages of eggs on the stream bottom for the males to fertilize. Once the female lays her eggs, her role in mating is finished. Some studies have found that males prefer to fertilize the eggs of red females. The female's red color is sending some sort of courtship signal to the male, but researchers don't know why males prefer red females.

A two-inch-long, freshwater fish called the stickleback also has a preference for red. Here, females appear to prefer depositing eggs in the nests of red males. But researchers don't know why this happens, either.

Scientists have studied the stickleback's courtship dance, though. During courtship, a male stickleback sets up a nest made of bits of plant matter. Then, he zigzags over the nest to attract passing females. If a female is interested, she stops and dances with the male, and the male swims around to display his nest more thoroughly. Successful courtship occurs when the female deposits her eggs in the nest and a male fertilizes them. Sometimes it is the nest-building male that fertilizes the eggs; other times a different male will sneak in to fertilize the eggs instead.

CRUSTACEAN COURTSHIP

Crustaceans include most sea creatures with outer shells and claws, such as crabs, lobsters, and shrimp. Crustaceans are arthropods, just like spiders. Like many of their fellow arthropods, crustaceans use physical gestures and movements to attract mates during courtship.

Crabs come in all shapes and sizes, and can live in saltwater, freshwater, or on land. As a result of this diversity, crab courtship is diverse as well. In general, many crabs wave their claws and dance to attract the attention of mates. Once a male and female find each other, the male will often carry the female on its back until the female molts, or sheds, her outer shell. While the female is forming her new, larger shell, she is ready to mate.

The courtship rituals of blue crabs of the Chesapeake Bay, off the coasts of Maryland and Virginia, are fairly typical. Courtship begins when a male stands up on his legs and waves his claws at a female. If interested, the female responds by waving her claws. The two touch claws and the male carries the female on his back for up to seven days, until she sheds her old shell. The two mate while her new shell is still soft.

THE IMPORTANCE OF SCHOOLS

A school of fish is comprised of many fish of the same variety swimming together. About 80% of fish swim in schools during some point in their lives. Scientists believe that fish school for a few reasons.

First, it takes less energy for a fish to swim in a group than to swim solo. Just as it is easier for cyclists to ride fast in groups, it is easier for fish to swim fast in groups. Each fish in a school creates a small current of water behind its tailfin. Individuals can, in theory, use these currents to help them swim easier and faster.

Second, schooling fish find safety in numbers. Scientists suggest that a small fish swimming in the open ocean has a better chance of being eaten if he swims by himself. Swimming together with a school, that same fish may avoid being eaten because some other fish gets eaten first.

Third, schooling is a way for fish to quickly find mates in the open sea. Groupers are a large-mouthed fish that spend most of their lives alone. When it's time to court and mate, they form schools of hundreds of fish for a few days.

Schooling isn't always a good thing. Schooling makes it easier for humans to find and catch large numbers of fish all at once. This sometimes depletes fish populations quickly. In the first half of the 1900s, sardine fishing was a thriving industry off the coast of northern California. But overfishing of sardine schools dropped the population from more than 4 million tons in the 1930s to just 5,000 tons by the 1970s. Schools of sardines started to disappear, and sardines started to school with anchovies instead.

More recently, sardine populations have recovered. In the late 1990s, experts estimated there were about 100,000 tons of sardines. Scientists have started to spot all-sardine schools once again.

A male blue crab waves its claws at a female for attention. If she waves back, the mating process begins.

Physical contact also is important during lobster courtship. Once a female lobster is admitted into the burrow of a male, a gentle boxing match begins. The two touch claws, and the male strokes the female lobster. She soon sheds her shell, and the lobsters mate. The female stays in the male's burrow after mating until her shell hardens. Then, she goes on her way.

CEPHALOPOD COURTSHIP

Cephalopods—octopuses, squids, and cuttlefish—are believed to be highly intelligent creatures. They have large brains and good eyesight, and can change the color and texture of their skin to match their surroundings. Cephalopods spend much of their time camouflaged to avoid predators. They also use their color-changing ability during courtship.

The cuttlefish is perhaps the most extreme example of a color-courting cephalopod. Often described as amazing, clever, and elaborate, the cuttlefish looks like a cross between an octopus and a squid. It has eight, long arms and a broad body, as well as W-shaped eyes.

Male cuttlefish often change color during courtship to attract the attention of females. Using all of his tentacles, a male puts on an elaborate display of colors for the female, ending with a vivid show of vibrant reds. If the show is successful, the male and female interlock their tentacles and mate.

A lively color show from a male cuttlefish can attract a potential mate.

Many types of octopus use color to attract mates during courtship. Usually, the male octopus begins the display. The color changes depend on the type of octopus. Some turn brown. Some turn red. Some display white polka dots.

Some scientists believe the cephalopods cannot see any color at all. Instead, they can detect brightness and patterns. So brightness, not color, is likely the real courtship tool that cephalopods are using.

Another type of cephalopod, an animal called the nautilus, is quite different from all the other cephalopods. It has an outer

THE NUMBERS GAME

Spawning is the process of releasing eggs into the water so that they can mix with sperm and grow into new animals. Spawning is a common way for fish and shellfish to mate. Fertilization, when the egg and sperm meet, happens completely outside the female's body, and the parent animals have little control over what happens.

For spawning to work, females must release large amounts of eggs into the water. Most of these eggs will never be fertilized; they are eaten by other creatures or swept away by currents. A few are fertilized by sperm and grow into offspring. The more eggs a female animal produces during spawning, the better her chances of reproducing.

Many female fish and shellfish produce thousands of eggs at a time. When an Atlantic salmon spawns, the female releases about 750 eggs for each pound of her body weight. So a 10-pound salmon releases about 7,500 eggs at a time.

The zebra mussel is a bivalve known for its ability to take over lakes. Female zebra mussels release about 40,000 eggs at a time. Sea stars release many more: about 50 mil-

shell, moves slowly in deep water, and does not change color. It is believed that the nautilus hasn't changed much in many millions of years. Nautilus courtship is not well understood.

BIVALVE COURTSHIP

The bivalves include scallops, clams, oysters, and mussels. None have heads, arms, or legs. Most adult bivalves never move; they attach themselves to hard surfaces under water, or bury themselves in dirt. As a result, bivalve courtship and mating don't

An Atlantic salmon jumps upstream in the River Ettrick in Scotland. Salmon and some sea turtles migrate back to the places they were born in order to reproduce; scientists believe they use magnetic fields in the Earth to find their way back to their spawning grounds.

lion eggs at a time. And many female clams release hundreds of millions of eggs each time they spawn. The more eggs, the better the chance of reproducing successfully.

really exist. Instead, bivalves release large numbers of eggs and sperm into the water, and leave the rest to chance. Some of the eggs and sperm meet. The sperm fertilize the eggs, and the next generation of bivalves begins.

Interestingly, some bivalves can be both male and female at the same time—with the ability to release eggs or sperm. Animals that do this are called **hermaphrodites**. Many bivalves are hermaphrodites. Others change from male to female, or from female to male, throughout their lives. Many oysters, for example, spend most of their young lives as males, and change into females later in life. Scientists are still studying how and when bivalves change sex. But courtship, in the case of bivalves, is not seen as a vital part of producing offspring.

ECHINODERM COURTSHIP

Echinoderms are a large group of saltwater animals that includes sea stars, sea urchins, and sea cucumbers. Most echinoderms have sticky tube feet that they use to move along hard surfaces. None have heads, or eyes. Perhaps as a result, echinoderm courtship is generally non-existent, or at least very simple.

In most cases, echinoderms release their eggs and sperm directly into the surrounding waters and allow fertilization to happen outside of the body. Courtship is not crucial because males and females do not choose mates. They release eggs and sperm when they are ready, regardless of other animals in the area.

Yet, in some cases, such as the courtship of the sea cucumber, there appears to be a little more happening. Sea cucumbers have long, leathery, cucumber-like bodies. They scavenge the seafloor for food. When a sea cucumber is ready to mate, some scientists suggest it releases chemicals into the water. These chemicals alert other sea cucumbers that mating is about to happen.

Once the chemical signals are sent and a partner has been found, both sea cucumbers arch their bodies like snakes about to

Courtship and mating among limbless sea cucumbers involves chemicals.

strike. Then they release their eggs or sperm into the water. In this case, there appears to be some form of courtship and mate choice occurring, though scientists are still studying what exactly happens.

MANY OFFSPRING

The courtship of fish and shellfish is diverse. Fertilization generally takes place outside of the body, so animals aren't always particular about mating partners. For fish and shellfish, it is more important to make as many offspring as possible so that some will survive and reproduce.

5

Reptile and Amphibian Courtship

REPTILES AND AMPHIBIANS include most of the animals that slither, hop, or crawl on the ground. Both reptiles and amphibians breathe air, but amphibians need water as well. Amphibians get up to 35% of their oxygen from water by absorbing it through their skin. Reptiles lay eggs that hatch into babies that look just like their parents, only smaller. Snakes, turtles, lizards, crocodiles, and alligators are reptiles. Amphibians lay eggs, too, but they must lay them in water, and the eggs hatch into babies that look nothing like their parents. As the babies develop, they undergo metamorphosis, changing from larva to adult. Frogs and salamanders are amphibians.

Reptiles and amphibians use many different courtship tools. Sound is a common courtship tool for these animals, as is touch. Most reptile and amphibian courtship rituals are hard to miss. Alligators and crocodiles bellow, cough, and blow bubbles; frogs croak and whine; lizards change color; snakes and turtles use touch.

REPTILES AND AMPHIBIAN SPECIES

There are about 7,000 species of reptiles, most of which are lizards and snakes. There are more than 6,000 species of amphibians. Reptiles and amphibians are cold-blooded animals called **ectotherms**. They maintain their body temperatures close to the temperature of the environment. When it's cold outside, a turtle gets cold. When it's warm outside, a turtle gets warm.

Reptiles and amphibians are primarily found in warm places, including forests, lakes, deserts, and tropical oceans. Because the temperature of these animals depends on the environment, they are very sensitive to temperature changes. Temperatures that are too cold or too hot cannot be tolerated. Although there are many different types of reptiles and amphibians, scientists suspect they are disappearing quickly because of rapid global warming.

ALLIGATORS AND CROCODILES

Alligators and crocodiles seem similar, but there are differences in how they look and where they live. Alligators tend to be darker in color, with wide noses. Their teeth don't show when they close their mouths. Alligators live in the southeastern United States. Crocodiles live all over the world. When it comes to courtship, both alligators and crocodiles use sound, but not in the same way.

Alligators use sound at several points during the courtship process. Males and females get one another's attention by bellowing, coughing, and blowing bubbles. They then might touch snouts, rub backs, and swim in circles together. Alligator courtship can last for hours.

Crocodiles also bellow and blow bubbles, but they use another type of sound during courtship as well. A crocodile can

A male alligator rises up and bellows to attract a female. Sound waves from the call cause vibrations in the water that also help attract the mate.

tighten and release its body underwater, creating a very low-toned sound called infrasound. Humans cannot hear infrasound, but some crocodiles use it during courtship to attract the attention of other crocodiles. They also may use it at other times, to scare off other crocodiles.

The courtship rituals of Florida's American crocodile are thought to be as complex as it gets for this group of animals. The male begins the process by slapping his head and vibrating his body. If the female is interested, she tilts her snout and her tail. The two blow bubbles, go swimming, and touch snouts.

TEMPERATURE-DEPENDENT SEX DETERMINATION

In most animals, the sex of the offspring is determined by its chromosomes and set from the very beginning. Nothing in the surrounding environment can change it. Reptiles are different. For most reptiles (including turtles, tortoises, alligators, and crocodiles), eggs develop into males or females depending on how warm they are kept in the nest.

When a female reptile fills a nest with eggs, none of the offspring in those eggs have yet to become males or females. The temperature of the eggs, as they develop over many weeks, will determine the sex of the offspring. Offspring in cooler eggs will become males. Those in warmer ones will become females.

(continues)

A green sea turtle lays eggs in its nest. The temperature of the nest will determine whether the eggs will produce males or females.

(continued)

This phenomenon is called **temperature-dependent sex determination**. It was discovered in the 1980s, but scientists don't yet completely understand how it works.

Some researchers suggest that females can control the sex of their offspring by building nests in warm or cold places. Others worry that climate change will affect the numbers of male and female reptiles born each year. Yet others argue that temperature-dependent sex determination could be used as a tool to help restore endangered animals.

Once courtship is successful, female alligators and crocodiles lay dozens of eggs in nests on the ground. Sometimes the females return to the nest to check on the eggs and help them hatch. The female's job usually ends when the eggs hatch and the offspring take to the water.

FROGS AND TOADS

There are more than 3,000 types of frogs and toads. Frogs tend to live in water and toads on land, but they are more similar than different. Almost all frogs and toads use sound as their primary tool during courtship. Go to the water's edge on a warm summer evening, and the croaks and ribbits of these common amphibians will likely be heard.

Scientists theorize that frogs and toads were the first land animals to develop and use sounds. Before them, most animals lived underwater and did not make sounds that traveled well in air. Today, male frogs and toads—not females—vocalize during courtship to attract females.

Sound is crucial in the courtship of frogs, and this male green tree frog's puffed throat is ready for croaking.

A typical evening of frog or toad courtship begins when the male calls out to surrounding females. These calls can take many different forms, including whines, chucks, peeps, croaks, and rib-bits. Each type of frog or toad has a distinct series of sounds. That helps a female choose a male of the correct species.

Tungara frogs, which live in Panama, have been well stud-ied. The males produce a specific series of courtship calls: one whine followed by up to six chucks. Females prefer the calls with the lowest tones. Usually, larger males make the lowest-toned calls. Scientists suspect that females use the calls to help them select the largest males.

LIZARDS

Lizards are one of the few reptiles that do not use sound as a primary tool during courtship. Instead, many lizards change colors. Chameleons, one of the best-known groups of lizards, are famous for this ability.

Contrary to popular belief, chameleons do not change color just to blend in to their surroundings. They typically change color to send signals to other chameleons—especially during courtship. Different types of chameleons can turn different shades. Depending on the kind of chameleon, the lizard's skin may turn pink, blue, red, orange, green, black, brown, or yellow.

Courtship often begins when a male chameleon bobs his head to get a female's attention. If she turns a dark color, she is not interested. If she turns a light, pale color, she is interested. The male usually responds with another color change. Scientists are still studying how chameleons communicate using colors.

The green anole is another type of lizard. It also can change color, and is often mistaken for a chameleon. A male green anole has a pink or red flap of skin on its neck, known as a dewlap. Males use dewlaps to court females. A male anole bobs his head, inflates the dewlap, and does push-ups to get a female's attention. In lizard courtship, color is the key.

SNAKES

Snakes are reptiles with worm-like body shapes. They have no legs, feet, hands, arms, or eyelids. They live on every continent except Antarctica. All snakes eat meat, but not all snakes are poisonous. In fact, only a small number of snakes are dangerous to humans. Most snakes don't see very well. They use smell and touch during courtship.

REPTILES AS PETS

In recent years, reptiles have become popular family pets. In 2005, about 11 million reptiles were kept as pets in this country—an increase of 2 million since 2003. That's a lot of reptiles.

Most people buy reptiles at pet stores. Before reptiles get to the pet store, they live in the wild. Trappers capture reptiles and either sell them to pet stores or keep them and sell their offspring to pet stores.

Over time, this hurts wild reptile populations and destroys habitats. Each year, about 2 million reptiles are brought into the United States from other countries so that people can buy them as pets. This removes reptiles from their natural habitats in other parts of the world. Unfortunately, many of these animals die within a year because they are not cared for correctly in captivity.

Many pet owners assume that reptiles are no-fuss, low-maintenance pets that largely fend for themselves in a home tank or aquarium, but this is not the case. Raising reptiles requires preparation and precaution. Disease is a major concern when keeping and touching pet reptiles.

Nearly all healthy reptiles carry bacteria that cause **salmonella**. These bacteria are a natural part of life for reptiles, but in humans the bacteria can cause diarrhea, vomiting, and fever. A salmonella infection can also lead to bigger health problems. The U.S. Centers for Disease Control and Prevention is part of the federal government. It estimates that about 74,000 people each year get salmonella sicknesses from reptiles and amphibians.

Owning a reptile as a pet might be fun for a while, but it also can cause problems. As a result, The Humane Society of the United States recommends that people not keep reptiles as pets. "Wild animals are best left in the wild where they belong," they say.

Snakes flick out their tongues to smell the air. Special receptors on a snake's tongue catch particles of scent. This helps the snake find food, avoid enemies, and locate mates during courtship.

Once a courting male and female identify each other with smell, they often use touch to continue the courtship. Some types of snakes twist their bodies together and lift themselves partway off the ground in a courtship dance. Others gently rub their bodies together before they mate.

TURTLES AND TORTOISES

Turtles and tortoises are reptiles that are difficult to confuse with any other animals. The outer shell of a turtle or tortoise is actually its rib cage and backbone. So, despite what is seen in cartoons, the shell cannot be removed. Turtles and tortoises have poor hearing and eyesight, so they use touch during courtship.

Turtles and tortoises live in rivers, ponds, lakes, and oceans, and on land near water. They have many courtship practices. Head bobbing, shell ramming, clawing, vibrating, and biting are fairly typical ones.

Courtship rituals of the loggerhead sea turtle involve a lot of biting and shell ramming. Courtship takes place at sea, often while turtles are migrating. A male sea turtle approaches a female and bites her neck or shoulder to get her attention. If the female is not interested, she swims deeper, away from the male. If courtship is successful, the two form a pair. During this process, other males may bite or ram the courting male with their shells, trying to get access to the female.

Many turtles commonly kept as pets, such as painted turtles and box turtles, have similarly physical courtship rituals.

Courting box turtles will bite, shove, and circle each other prior to mating.

USING SHARP SENSES

For reptiles and amphibians, courtship rituals take advantage of an animal's sharper senses. Animals with bad eyesight, such as turtles, alligators, and frogs, use touch and sound to court one another. Animals with good eyesight, such as lizards, use color. Nature uses what works.

6

Bird Courtship

BIRDS ARE ANIMALS that have feathers and beaks, and lay eggs with hard shells. Of all the different animal courtship rituals, bird courtship is perhaps the best studied. Birds are fairly easy to watch in the wild, and they're interesting, too.

Many birds use songs and colors during courtship. Songs are often used to attract the attention of potential mates and to communicate. The male nightingale is famous for singing night and day to attract a mate. Male birds also often display brightly colored feathers to attract the attention of females. The male peacock maintains the ultimate collection of colorful feathers. The feathers seem to serve no purpose except to make him attractive during courtship.

THE BIRD POPULATION

There are about 10,000 different varieties of birds. They range in size from tiny hummingbirds to giant ostriches, and they live in all corners of the globe.

Birds are closely related to reptiles, such as snakes and lizards. Although they appear quite different, birds and reptiles share some qualities. For one thing, they both lay eggs with

The courtship dance of red-crowned cranes involves prancing, leaps, bows, and loud unison calls. The courting cranes also throw sticks and other objects into the air with their beaks and then stab at the objects as they fall back down.

shells. Both birds and reptiles share a common ancestor: the dinosaur.

Birds are social animals. Their courtship rituals are filled with songs, cooperation, and long-term care for their young.

DUCKS

Duck is a common name for many types of birds, all closely related to geese and swans. Ducks live, feed, and mate near fresh or salt water in many parts of the world. Male ducks are usually more colorful than females. Males use distinctive calls to attract mates during courtship. Because ducks are fairly easy to find and watch, much is known about duck courtship.

The courtship of the common mallard is easy to study and observe. The mallard displays both of the common duck courtship tools: feather colors and distinctive calls.

Male mallards have bright green feathers on their heads. They have gray and black body feathers. Female mallards have brown and black speckled feathers. Scientists suspect that these color differences help birds identify their own species and help make the males more attractive to females.

The more colorful male mallard (*left*) looks very different than the female mallard.

Male mallards often begin courtship with an attention-getting song and dance. A courting male will shake its head and tail, raise its breast and wing tips, and arch its neck. All the while, the male is singing, whistling, and grunting. In response, female mallards will call to tempt males into fighting with other males or females. They may be testing the males to see which is the strongest.

The entire courtship display is common but brief, sometimes lasting only a few minutes. A male and female mallard will pair up and mate rather quickly, and may mate again with other partners during the mating season. Most types of ducks mate during warmer months when ponds are thawed and food is plentiful.

Different types of ducks court one another at about the same time each year. Yet, each type of duck has its own colors, dances, and songs. Scientists suspect these differences help ducks mate with ducks of their own species.

Eiders, shovelers, wigeons, and teals are other groups of ducks that use similar courtship tools.

PENGUINS

Many birds live everywhere in the world except for the southernmost continent: Antarctica. There, penguins rule.

Penguins spend about half their lives on land and half in the water. They cannot fly; they waddle and slide over land. In the water, penguins mainly swim to find food. Penguin courtship involves a lot of song and dance. Yet, unlike many birds, many penguins are thought to be **monogamous**. That means they court and mate with the same partner every year.

The Emperor penguin is the largest and perhaps best-studied penguin. When it is time to reproduce, usually in March or April, Emperors leave the sea and travel more than 50 miles

Adélie penguins stretch upward and thrust their beaks outward in a courtship display.

(90 km) over land to the same location. There, they all gather to court and mate.

Courtship begins when a male Emperor penguin calls out to find the female he courted in years past. The male will stand in one place and call loudly for a few seconds. Then he will move to a new place and call again. He repeats this pattern until he finds his female or a new mating partner who returns his call. After the female eventually lays an egg, the male and female take turns caring for the egg—and, once it's hatched, the chick—together until the young penguin can stand on the ice and care for itself.

Other penguins, including the smaller Adélie penguins, have similar courtship rituals. Males and females identify each other from year to year with their calls, and males stretch out their necks and thrust out their beaks in courtship displays prior to mating.

Scientists suspect many penguins are monogamous because their time to court and mate is limited by weather. Each year, there is only a short time when it is warm enough to successfully raise an egg. Penguins have no time to waste in finding or fighting over mates. Choosing the same mate each year is thought to be easier.

That said, penguin partners do not always mate monogamously. Sometimes males and females cannot find each other fast enough to pair up; other times a partner will not return to mate at all, so the penguin finds a new partner to rear its young.

King penguins, chinstrap penguins, rockhopper penguins, and African penguins are other common types of penguins with similar courtship tactics.

PHEASANTS

The pheasants are a group of chicken-like birds. Quails, grouse, turkeys, and partridges are some common types of pheasants. These birds are known for strong sexual dimorphism. Many male pheasants have brightly colored feathers or other

SENDING SIGNALS

Imagine trying to listen to someone in a loud, crowded room. The person's mouth moves. Sounds come out. A message is being sent, but it cannot be understood. There is too much noise and distraction.

Many birds and other animals face this challenge when they sing to attract a mate. They are trying to send a signal, but it does not always get through as intended. Songs from other animals and environmental factors affect how the signal is heard.

Some scientists focus on how animal signals are sent and heard by other animals.

Researchers record birdsongs during courtship and then study how fast the songs are, how often the bird sings, and in what direction the bird is singing, among other things. Researchers also may study how those songs are heard. For example, sound travels differently in a summer forest (in which the trees have leaves) than in a winter forest (In which the leaves have dropped).

In many cases, the loudest songs come from the largest animals. Sending a loud signal can be critical to successful courtship.

decorations, including fancy tails, unlike most females. These decorations are important during courtship.

During courtship, males do their best to show their health and strength by displaying their bright colors and decorations. Female pheasants are attracted to vibrant colors and elaborate feather displays.

Peacocks are the classic example of sexual dimorphism in pheasants. Male peacocks have bright blue and green feathers. They can fan out these long feathers to attract the attention of females. Female peacocks, sometimes called peahens, also have feathers that fan out, but the feathers usually are duller and shorter than the males' feathers.

Scientists have found little use for male peacock feathers other than to attract attention. Males use their feathers primarily during courtship. Females seem to display their feathers as warning signals for their offspring and other females.

Male peacocks have fancier feathers in order to attract the attention of females. Even male white peacocks, like this one, have longer, brighter feathers than female counterparts.

SEABIRDS

Seabird is a non-scientific term that includes all birds that live at sea. Seabirds live near oceans, on islands, or fly from one place to another in the ocean. Although these birds belong to several different scientific groups, they have similar lifestyles. Their courtship rituals are also similar.

Most seabirds court one another and raise offspring in groups called colonies. The largest colonies can include one million birds. Colonies are often found on protected, rocky islands or coastlines. Seabirds come to colonies only to mate and nest. These birds don't have many offspring in their lifetimes, but they put a lot of time and energy into caring for the offspring that they do have.

The courtship rituals of the albatrosses are typical of many seabirds. Albatrosses live throughout the world's oceans. Many are endangered.

When albatrosses are ready to mate, they return to the colony in which they were born to find a partner. These birds are monogamous; they mate with the same bird every season.

The courtship rituals vary between the different types of albatross. All courtship rituals include dancing and calling. The well-studied Laysan albatross of the North Pacific Ocean performs a series of 25 different poses while calling to its mate. The giant wandering albatross of the Southern Ocean also displays and calls to its mate during courtship.

Gulls, terns, boobies, auks, and petrels are other common groups of seabirds that court in colonies.

SONGBIRDS

Songbirds are a group of birds with highly developed voices. They can produce many different song-like notes and tones. They use

CUCKOO BIRDS

Cuckoo birds are a large group of songbirds famous for their courtship calls. They also are known for their sneaky parenting techniques.

The common cuckoo lives in Europe and Asia. It has the distinctive "cuck-oo" call that is mimicked in cuckoo clocks. Each species of cuckoo has its own distinctive call, but scientists are interested in studying cuckoos for another fascinating reason.

Once courtship is complete and the female cuckoo is ready to lay her eggs, she does not lay them in her own nest. Instead, she lays them in the nest of another bird. After the eggs hatch, the unsuspecting mother feeds and cares for the cuckoo babies along with her own offspring.

(continues)

During courtship, a male Diederik cuckoo will feed caterpillars to its mate.

> *(continued)*
>
> Often, the cuckoo babies are much larger than the other baby birds. The cuckoos sometimes kick out the other babies in order to get more food.
>
> The female cuckoo's behavior is called **cuckolding**. Over time, female cuckoos' eggs have evolved to look almost identical to the other eggs in the cuckolded nest. The nesting birds do not recognize the difference of the cuckoo eggs, and they raise the offspring as their own. The cuckoos get healthy offspring without having to do much work.
>
> Such cuckolding behavior is well studied in cuckoos and other birds, but it also occurs in some species of fish and mammals.

their songs to mark territories, identify themselves, and attract mates.

Many birds use calls during courtship, but these calls are often simple and repetitive. They are used to sound warning alarms or attract the attention of other birds. Songbirds' songs are more complex. Female songbirds sometimes use males' songs to help judge the health of the males. Male songbirds sing to compete with one another.

Male nightingales, for example, are famous for their singing abilities. They sing day and night, belting out a series of whistles, shrills, and gurgles that are often pleasing to the human ear. Female nightingales choose mates with songs that interrupt less aggressive, quieter birds. The louder a male's song is, the better his chance of finding a mate.

Other songbirds use songs as their main tools during courtship as well. Yet, not all songs are pleasing to humans, and not all songbirds are small, delicate birds like the nightingales.

The black-capped chickadee, seen here, has slower and lower-pitched calls after breeding season. It will also be larger and have more white on the edge of its wing.

Crows and ravens, for example, are considered songbirds. These large, black birds are believed to be very intelligent. They can mimic human voices and other animals, and are able to produce dozens of complex sounds. Scientists have learned that crows and ravens use songs to attract mates during courtship, but their sounds and courtship behaviors are still being studied.

Chickadees, cuckoos, warblers, swallows, and sparrows are other examples of common songbirds that sing during courtship.

WOODPECKERS

Woodpeckers are tree-loving birds. They get their name because they peck at dead trees and other surfaces. Woodpeckers usually peck in search of insects for food, or to communicate with other woodpeckers. During courtship, male woodpeckers often tap on trees to mark their territory and attract females.

The red-bellied woodpecker is a common resident of the eastern United States. Males create a drumming sound when

The noisy drumming of the red-bellied woodpecker in the United States is typically the sound of these birds trying to find a mate.

courting females, who usually respond with a similar drumming sound if interested. The drumming takes place anywhere that makes good sound, including on trees, telephone poles, house gutters and sidings. This is fairly typical courting behavior for common woodpeckers in the United States.

Other woodpeckers are more mysterious. Little is known of the courtship behavior of the large, rare, ivory-billed woodpecker of the southeastern United States. This woodpecker actually may be extinct. One was supposedly seen and videotaped in Arkansas in 2005, but none have been seen since. Scientists suspect that the courtship rituals of the ivory-billed woodpecker focused on close, physical contact, rather than on making sounds. But the facts will likely never be known.

MUCH MORE TO LEARN

Scientists have seen and documented courtship in many types of birds. Birds can be easy and interesting to watch. Yet, there are many birds, and little is known about courtship in some species. Scientists continue to study bird courtship all over the world.

Mammal Courtship

MAMMALS INCLUDE ALL ANIMALS that have hair and produce milk to feed their babies. Housecats, killer whales, lions, and humans are all mammals. Some courtship rituals in mammals have been well studied. Others are still mostly a mystery.

Mammals use physical combat and scent during courtship. Males often fight over females. Many male mammals have evolved special characteristics for fighting. Scientists also know that scent signals are important during mammal courtship. Female rhinoceroses give off a courtship scent; so do many female monkeys.

Mammals may use dance, color, and sound during courtship as well. Mammals that live in water often use touch and sound.

THE MAMMAL POPULATION

Mammals are one of the most familiar groups of animals, but they are not the largest. There are only about 5,000 species of mammals on the planet. Within the class of mammals there is a huge amount of diversity.

The smallest mammals include some shrews and bats. They weigh as much as one teaspoon of sugar (about 0.1 ounces, or 3 grams). The largest mammals are also the largest animals. The blue whale can weigh more than 350 pounds (160,000 kilograms); it is about as heavy as a Boeing 747 airplane. This makes it 53 million times heavier than the smallest bats and shrews. Mammals truly come in all sizes.

Mammals are found on all continents, in all oceans, and on many islands. The courtship rituals of some hoofed mammals, marine mammals, predators, small mammals, and primates are described here.

HOOFED MAMMALS

Hoofed mammals include horses, deer, llamas, pigs, goats, antelopes, and rhinoceroses, among others. Scientifically, all of these animals aren't necessarily related. Still, they all share a similar foot structure: a foot with a hard, bone-like toe, or hoof.

A male and female moose nuzzle together in Anchorage, Alaska. The bigger the antlers, the stronger a male will look to a female.

These mammals are known as **ungulates**. There are many rituals of ungulate courtship, and many involve physical combat and scent.

MAMMAL MOMS AND BABIES

Mammal mothers have a limited number of chances to produce healthy offspring. Fish and spiders can produce thousands of offspring at a time, but mammal mothers give birth to many fewer babies. They also use more energy caring for the babies once they are born. The number of babies that a female mammal has in her lifetime depends on two things: the length of **gestation** and how long she raises her young.

The gestation period is the amount of time a female mammal carries the young in her body. For humans, the gestation period is about 40 weeks. During this time, the baby grows and develops so that it can survive outside the mother's body. In general, larger mammals have longer gestation periods. Female elephants are pregnant for nearly two years before giving birth.

Compared with fish or insects, it takes female mammals a long time to grow and give birth to offspring. It also takes mammals a long time to raise those offspring once they are born. Baby mammals are dependent on their mothers for milk. Some young mammals—including cats, dogs, bears, and humans—cannot move on their own right away. They need a mother's protection. On the other hand, many ungulates and marine mammals can walk or swim right away, and they can move around on their own. Their mothers still give them milk and protect them.

Baby bears may stay with their mothers for only one year; some baby whales stay with their mothers for six years or more. The length of the gestation period, combined with the time it takes to raise the young, means that female mammals spend a lot of time raising just a few babies.

Moose are the largest members of the deer family, and their courtship rituals are similar to other deer. Moose, like many ungulates, use both physical combat and scent during courtship. In

On average, an elephant stays with its mother for about 16 years. This African elephant mother stands over her one-day-old baby.

the fall mating season, female moose court males by giving off a strong scent and calling with deep voices. Male moose sometimes rely on physical combat.

Male moose begin growing antlers in early summer. By courtship season, males use these impressive antlers to show off their size and sometimes to fight other males.

A male moose assesses the size of another male by looking at the antlers. In a male-male standoff, the moose with smaller antlers will usually back down before there is any physical contact. But sometimes the males may push each other around a bit. Head-to-head combat can cause the antlers to become entangled. If this happens, both moose usually die. At the end of the mating season, male moose shed their antlers.

A different sort of ungulate, the rhinoceros, also uses scent and physical contact during courtship. When a female rhino is ready to mate, she gives off a scent in her urine and dung. Males use their horns or teeth to fight each other for access to the females.

Once offspring are born, ungulate mothers care for them for about two years. During this time, the babies learn to find food, avoid danger, and fend for themselves. When a mother has another baby, her older offspring will become independent.

MARINE MAMMALS

The marine mammals are a group of animals that spend their lives in or near the ocean. Polar bears, seals, manatees, otters, dolphins, and whales are marine mammals. Because marine mammals spend much of their time at sea, their courtship rules and rituals are not always well documented or well understood.

Little is known about the courtship behaviors of many whales, such as blue whales and beaked whales. These animals are difficult to find and watch. By contrast, people often can see the courtship of other whales, such as the northern right whale, at the ocean's surface.

Many marine mammals use physical size and sound during courtship. Male elephant seals use physical size to compete for access to females. Once each year, elephant seals gather in one place to court and mate. The males arrive first. They use sound, body size, and the occasional fight to stake out territories. The largest males establish the largest territories. As a result, they court and mate with the most females. Other male marine mammals, including some types of dolphins and manatees, form large groups that pursue females during courtship.

Perhaps the best-known marine mammal that uses sound during courtship is the humpback whale. Male humpback whales sing long, complex songs. Sometimes the songs last for 24 hours. Females can make sounds, but they do not sing. At first, scientists assumed that male humpbacks sang to attract females. However, singing males have been observed attracting the attention of other males, so courtship may not be the only purpose of the songs. Scientists suspect the songs may also be important for navigation, identification, and intimidation of other whales.

PREDATORS

Predators often eat other animals for food (small predators sometimes get eaten by larger predators, too). Predators are a diverse and widespread group of creatures. Predator mammals include weasels, wolves, elephant seals, bears, and cats. Some predators are social animals that live in large groups. Others are solitary creatures that pair up only during mating season. A predator's courtship rituals are linked with its social nature.

In social predator societies, large males often compete for females during courtship. In these cases, large male body size is often a big advantage. Lions live in groups known as prides. Usually, the largest, strongest male lion is the leader of the pride, and he has his choice of courting and mating with the females in his group.

Lions court and mate only with other pride members. Yet, within a pride, a male will court many females, and a female will mate with many males. Part of the reason for this is that lions aren't very successful at getting pregnant. Scientists estimate that lions must mate 3,000 times for every cub that survives more than one year. Lions mate often, so courtship is quick.

Wolves are another example of predators that live in groups, but their courtship practices are different from those of lions. Wolves live as monogamous pairs. Once a male and female pair is established, it stays together for life. The pair usually produces many offspring. As a result, gray wolf courtship happens only when a wolf is seeking a mate for the first time, or when a wolf's mate has died and it needs to find a new one.

Gray wolves live in groups called packs. Within the pack, there is one male leader and one female leader. These are the alpha wolves. They are the only two wolves in the pack that will mate and have babies. All the other pack members will help care for these babies.

The alpha wolves are not always the largest ones. Some wolves choose to leave their birth packs and set out on their own. These wolves may form pairs and establish territories, eventually beginning a new pack together in which they are the leaders.

Because solitary predators live by themselves, they need ways to find mates. Predators have excellent senses of hearing, eyesight, and smell. These senses, especially the sense of smell, come into play during courtship.

A male and a female lion of the same pride lie together.

Bears are solitary predators with sensitive noses. During courtship, the female attracts a male with chemical signals. Many solitary weasels, badgers, and skunks also use these chemical signals, which are called pheromones.

SMALL MAMMALS

Rodents, rabbits, moles, and shrews are all classic examples of small mammals. Many of the classic, small prey animals live in groups in protected places, often underground.

A male gray wolf (*left*) greets a female gray wolf. If they become an established pair, wolves couple together for life.

Rodents are the largest scientific group of mammals. There are about 2,000 different species of rodents. Each species has slightly different courtship rules and rituals.

The standard city rat lives in social groups with dominant male leaders. These male leaders court and mate with many different females. Beavers, on the other hand, live as monogamous pairs for life. Scientists don't know how beavers conduct their courtship, but an adult beaver rarely lives alone for long.

For many small mammals, such as rabbits and porcupines, scent plays a key role in courtship. Rabbits smell out potential mates. Female porcupines court males using scent in their urine.

PRIMATES

Primates include lemurs, monkeys, and apes. Most primates live in social groups and are considered intelligent animals. As is true of many mammals, size and scent are the key tools used during primate courtship. Primates also have sexual dimorphism, which means the males are often larger than the females. In some cases, males can be twice as large as females. Males and females often urinate or leave a scent to court one another and show interest. Unlike many mammals, primates have good vision, so color is another tool used during courtship.

Lemurs are good examples of primates that use scent during courtship. A male lemur will smell the urine of a female. If the male is interested, he then wafts his specially scented tail at the female. If she accepts the display, she may curl her tail to invite the male to mate. Lorises and marmosets also use scent signals during courtship.

Baboons are monkeys that use color during courtship. The rear ends of female baboons swell and turn bright red when the females are ready to mate.

THE BALANCE OF MALES AND FEMALES

Among most types of animals, there are about the same number of males as females. In the past, scientists thought this happened because of chance. Now, however, scientists think there is more to this fact.

It seems that females that mate with attractive or dominant males tend to produce more male offspring. Humans are no exception.

Research at the United States Military Academy in West Point, New York, found that women married to high-ranking officers had more sons than would be expected by chance alone. Studies of U.S. presidents, vice presidents, and cabinet secretaries found that these dominant males tended to produce more sons than daughters. For example, 70% of the offspring from the first 20 U.S. presidents were sons. If having males or females were due only to chance, then about 50% of these offspring should be sons.

Some scientists suggest that dominant males produce more male offspring because, in theory, these males could produce many more offspring themselves than daughters could. A female mammal can produce a limited number of offspring in her lifetime. Yet, if they mate with multiple females, male mammals can produce many more offspring.

Gorillas and orangutans, which are species of ape, are good examples of sexual dimorphism. Male gorillas, often called silverbacks, easily can be twice the size of females. Similarly, male orangutans can be twice the size of female orangutans. The larger males are often the most successful during courtship.

Scientifically, humans are considered apes as well. But the courtship of humans has long been influenced by human culture.

DIVERSITY AMONG MAMMALS

Many mammals use scent as a primary courtship tool, but mammal courtship depends on the social nature of each species and

Scent plays a big part in the courtship of ring tailed lemurs.

where it lives in the world. Humans are the prime example of a mammal with courtship rituals that are heavily influenced by social rules and culture.

How Courtship Research is Gathered

MANY HOURS OF RESEARCH and observation go into learning about the rituals of animal courtship. There are as many different ways to study animal courtship as there are animals to study. Some scientists study courtship in the laboratory, while others observe how animals act in nature. Many do both.

Scientists who study animal courtship come from many different scientific areas. Some are trained as ecologists or biologists. Others are trained as zoologists or psychologists. Each of them has a desire to document and understand animal courtship behavior.

What follows are profiles of several scientists who study animal courtship. They come from different places, work in different locations, and study different animals—but they all are contributing to the scientific understanding of animal courtship today.

INSECT AND ARACHNID COURTSHIP RESEARCHER: MAYDIANNE ANDRADE

Maydianne Andrade studies the courtship and mating rituals of Australian redback spiders, close relatives of black widows.

Nearly all of her work is conducted in the laboratory, where she pairs up courting spiders to see what they do and why they do it.

Redback spiders are interesting because the large, black female (about 0.5 inches long, or 1.3 centimeters long) eats the smaller male (only about 0.1 inches long, or 3 mm long) while the two spiders are mating. When one animal eats another during courtship or mating, it is called **sexual cannibalism**. Many

Researcher Maydianne Andrade studies a redback spider on its web in a web frame. The female spider created the web, on which she and the male will later mate and have meals.

spiders and some insects, including the praying mantis, practice sexual cannibalism.

What's unusual about the redback spider is that the male appears to offer himself as a meal for the female. During mating, the male redback spider somersaults onto the female's fangs. He is often being digested during mating. The female clearly benefits from this mating trick: She gets a mate as well as a meal. Andrade has discovered that the male benefits, too.

Andrade keeps about 10,000 redback spiders in her laboratory. When she wants to learn about redback spider mating, she lets them mate and watches what happens.

In one study, Andrade and her colleagues recorded spider mating with a special, zoom-lens camera. They also measured the males and females using a microscope. They kept track of how long each mating lasted and recorded whether the male was eaten. (Sometimes the female lets the male live.)

They also measured the amount of sperm (the male reproductive cells that are inserted in the female during mating) that was left inside each female.

The study found that when a male redback spider was eaten, he injected more sperm into the female. Other studies found that males that were eaten mated for twice as long as uneaten males and fathered twice as many offspring with that female. A chance to father a lot of offspring is the ultimate goal for the mating male. He gets to pass on his traits to the next generation of redback spiders.

However, the male redback spider does more than get eaten. It can take many minutes for the female to eat the male. While she is eating, the male has time to insert a plug into the female redback spider. This keeps other males from injecting sperm. The plug increases the male's chances of fathering more offspring.

At the same time, Andrade and her graduate student, Jeff Stoltz, found that males are able to pinch off parts of their body while being eaten by females. Andrade suggests that this protects important parts of the body, such as the heart, so that the male can survive longer and inject more sperm.

Andrade began her work in animal courtship studying biology at the University of Toronto, Mississauga, and Cornell University, Ithaca, New York. She is currently an associate professor in Ecology & Evolutionary Biology at the University of Toronto, Scarborough.

FISH COURTSHIP RESEARCHER: CONSTANTINO MACÍAS GARCIA

Constantino Macías Garcia studies mating in freshwater fish. His research begins in the laboratory, where he can manipulate and watch fish courtship. Then he goes to the field to confirm what he's seen in the lab. Macías Garcia is interested in how, through sexual selection, fish have developed special fin colors and designs to attract mates during courtship.

THE ANIMAL BEHAVIOR SOCIETY

For young people interested in a career studying animal courtship, the Animal Behavior Society (ABS) is a good place to look for information and expertise. ABS was founded in 1964 to encourage and promote the study of animal behavior. It is made up of scientists actively studying this topic. The ABS publishes a scientific journal of research papers called *Animal Behaviour*. It also publishes a newsletter with job and fellowship announcements in the field.

According to Gil Rosenthal, the Public Affairs Chair for ABS and a courtship researcher at Texas A&M University, there are no colleges with programs specifically tailored to the study of animal courtship, but several schools have strong concentrations of experts in animal behavior. These schools are listed below.

College	Departments
Cornell University, Ithaca, NY	Department of Ecology and Evolutionary Biology
Indiana University, Bloomington, IN	Evolution, Ecology and Behavior Program
Princeton University, Princeton, NJ	Department of Ecology and Evolutionary Biology
State University of New York, Stony Brook, NY	Department of Ecology and Evolution
Texas A&M University, College Station, TX	Faculty of Ecology and Evolutionary Biology
University of Arizona, Tucson, AZ	Department of Ecology and Evolutionary Biology
University of California, Davis, Davis, CA	Section of Evolution and Ecology
University of California, Riverside, Riverside, CA	Department of Biology
University of Florida, Gainesville, FL	Department of Zoology
University of Illinois at Urbana-Champaign, Urbana, IL	Program in Ecology and Evolutionary Biology
University of Minnesota, Twin Cities, MN	Department of Ecology, Evolution, and Behavior
University of North Carolina, Chapel Hill, NC	Evolution, Ecology, and Organismal Biology
University of Texas at Austin, Austin, TX	Section of Integrative Biology
University of Wisconsin, Madison, WI	Botany, Zoology, Wildlife Ecology

One group of fish that Macías Garcia studies is called the Goodeinae. These fish are about 2 to 10 inches long (5 cm to 25 cm long). They live in the fresh waters of central Mexico and come in dozens of different varieties. Male Goodeinae from several varieties have yellow stripes on their tail fins that look like food.

Macías Garcia and other scientists say the yellow fin stripes originally evolved to look like wriggling worms, enticing females to approach for a meal. Yet, instead of a meal, the female would

Researcher Constantino Macías Garcia works in his office at the Institute for Ecology of the National Autonomous, which is part of the University of Mexico in Mexico City. On his computer screen is a picture of a hand-made traditional tile that depicts the yellow stripe on a male fish's tail, which he says shows the local craftspeople have long recognized the unique stripe on some fish species.

end up mating with the male. The yellow stripes acted like a courtship trap.

To better understand female fish responses to the yellow stripes, Macías Garcia and his colleagues tested fish in the laboratory. The scientists presented each female with two males: one with a yellow tail stripe and one without. The female could see both males, but the males could not see each other.

When they allowed the males to show only their tails, the scientists discovered that the females of some varieties no longer fall for the yellow-tail trap. Females of varieties where males have a bright yellow stripe do not attempt to bite the tails of the males in search of food, as was the case in varieties that have light yellow stripes or no stripes at all. Instead the females of bright-tailed varieties pay attention to the color in a different way.

Macías Garcia and his colleagues concluded that the females are attracted to the males with the brightest yellow tails, perhaps because the tails are now signs of good male health. Not because they are looking for a meal. Only the healthiest males can afford to maintain the bright yellow tail stripe. They should therefore produce the healthiest offspring. The yellow tail stripe is no longer a trap for many varieties of Goodeinae, but it is still a tool used in courtship.

Much of Macías Garcia's work involves experimenting with fish behaviors in the laboratory. He has studied many different kinds of fish, including the Amarillo fish. He showed that in Amarillo fish, ornaments—such as bright colors or large fins—are costly to maintain because they can interfere with escaping from predators.

Once Macías Garcia understands a behavior in the laboratory, he double-checks his observations by watching the fish in their natural environment. "It is always necessary to go back to the field and test some of the possible consequences of what one sees in captivity," he explains.

Macías Garcia is currently a researcher based at the National University of Mexico's Ecology Institute. In the future, Macías Garcia plans to study how the courtship rituals of **introduced animals** affect the courtship of **native animals**.

SHELLFISH COURTSHIP RESEARCHER: DENISE POPE

Denise Pope studies how fiddler crabs use signals to communicate during courtship. She does not do experiments in a laboratory. Instead, she watches the crabs in their natural environment.

Fiddler crabs are small crabs; the biggest are just two 2 inches (5 cm) across. They live in the intertidal zones of sandy shores, which are exposed to air at low tide. At high tide, they are underwater. Thousands of fiddler crabs can live on any given shore, each in its own sandy burrow.

Fiddler crab males have one large, fiddle-shaped claw that they use to make signals and attract the attention of females. A male fiddler crab will wave his large claw at a female. If she's interested, the female will walk up to the male. She might go into his burrow for a minute, and then come out. Female fiddler crabs will visit the burrows of many waving males before selecting one for mating.

Pope seeks to learn more about how males use their claws to communicate during courtship. She has traveled to North Carolina, Texas, Panama, and Portugal. Since 2006, Pope has been studying the fiddler crabs in Kino Bay, Mexico. She says the crabs are ideal animals to study in nature because they are "active, abundant, and amenable to both behavioral observations and experimental manipulations."

A male fiddler crab attempts to attract a female to his sandy burrow by waving his giant claw. Scientists have learned that there may be sexual conflict among fiddler crabs, in which some males force females into their burrows.

In a recent study on the Kino Bay crabs, Pope and student Brian Haney saw an unusual courtship behavior called male directing. In male directing, a male fiddler crab uses his giant claw to maneuver a female into his burrow so he can mate with her. Pope and Haney wanted to understand this behavior. They wondered: Are females allowing themselves to be directed by males that they prefer? Or are males overpowering females by force?

To answer their questions, the scientists watched the directing behaviors of the male fiddler crabs for many hours. They caught and measured the successful and unsuccessful directing males. Pope and Haney found that the successful males were larger and heavier than the females that were directed. However, they did not find any evidence that successful males were any healthier than unsuccessful males.

Pope says this is evidence that males overpower females during courtship. The large males are the strongest crabs on the beach, but not necessarily the healthiest. When male crabs use their body size to overpower a female and outcompete other males, says Pope, it is evidence of **sexual conflict**.

A sexual conflict occurs when males and females have different goals during courtship and mating. These situations are common in the animal world, but this is the first time sexual conflict has been found in fiddler crabs. Still, most of the time, female fiddler crabs choose their own mates.

Pope began her career studying fiddler crabs while earning a doctoral degree in zoology at Duke University. This work was completed when Pope was an assistant professor at Trinity University's Department of Biology in San Antonio, Texas.

REPTILE COURTSHIP RESEARCHER: MICHAEL J. RYAN

Mike Ryan has studied the tungara, or mud puddle, frog for nearly 30 years. The tungara frog lives in Central America and the Caribbean. It is small; the largest ones are only 1.5 inches (3.8 cm) long. Ryan spends hours observing tungara frogs in the wild, and then makes sense of his observations in the laboratory.

When Ryan first began his research, little was known about this frog. But today, Ryan and dozens of researchers journey to Panama every summer to study tungara frogs. They have learned a lot about tungara frog courtship.

Like most frogs, male tungara frogs croak and call to attract females. But unlike most frogs, the tungara males have two

Scientists have found that the brain of the tiny female tungara frog—shown here on the tip of a pencil eraser—responds best to deeper, more complex male frog calls.

different kinds of calls: simple calls and complex calls. Ryan has been trying to figure out which calls females prefer and why.

Each summer, Ryan and other researchers record the court-ship calls of the tungara males in the wild. They also experiment to see how female frogs respond to recorded male frog calls.

Over the years, these scientists have learned that the female tungara frogs prefer the deeper, more complex calls of male frogs. Deep calls help males attract females, but they also can attract predators: bats. A calling male tungara frog risks being eaten when it tries to court females.

Generally speaking, says Ryan, the larger, healthier males can produce the deep calls. At first, it looked as if females used the calls to find the biggest males. This might be because they were trying to have large, healthy offspring.

Ryan worked with neuroscientists (scientists that study the brain) to study the female preference for deep and complex calls. In the laboratory, the group discovered that the brains of female tungara frogs are most sensitive to deeper sounds. Female frogs are programmed to respond best to big frogs. This wiring probably evolved over many thousands of years. The females that were wired this way mated with large males, and had larger, healthier offspring that survived better. Eventually, the "wiring" for choosing large males spread throughout the entire species.

Ryan began his work in science as a high school biology teacher, and then went on to study animal behavior at Rutgers University in Newark, New Jersey. Since his professional research career began, Ryan has published nearly 150 papers on his work with the tungara frogs of Panama.

Ryan is currently an advisor to approximately eight graduate students and two undergraduates. He is professor of zoology at the University of Texas in Austin, Texas. Ryan works with the students to better understand different aspects of the life of the tungara frog. He helps students form and develop research ideas of their own.

Each summer, Ryan takes field assistants to Panama to assist in the research. For more information on working on the project, visit Ryan's website at http://www.sbs.utexas.edu/ryan.

BIRD COURTSHIP RESEARCHER: GAIL PATRICELLI

Gail Patricelli studies the many different signals—such as color, sounds, and scent—that animals use to communicate in the wild. She also studies how these signals evolve over time. Most of her work involves studying birds in their natural environments, including songbirds and sage-grouse.

The male sage-grouse uses multiple signals to attract the attention of females during courtship. He will strut around, inflating and deflating two yellow air sacs in his chest. He also makes a distinct puff-up, breathy sound. Scientists suspect that females prefer males that make the loudest sounds. To test this idea, they need to measure how loud a male's signals sound to a female sage-grouse while she is darting around in a pack of males.

To understand what the female sage-grouse sees and hears, Patricelli and her colleagues built a robotic, remote-controlled, stuffed female grouse that can run on rails around a courtship area. The robot can record the sights and sounds of the males. Using the remote control, Patricelli can "respond" to male sage-grouse and see what happens. Patricelli calls the robot her "fembot."

Patricelli plans to use the fembot to help her understand how a male sage-grouse directs his sounds to be heard by females. Just as a human can turn to direct the sound of his or her voice, a male sage-grouse can turn to direct the sound of his courtship puff. This may make him sound louder and more attractive to females.

In one study in Montana, scientists discovered a male sage-grouse that successfully courted 169 females in one season. In the same group of birds, other males failed to successfully court even one female. Patricelli hopes the fembot will help her understand why one male makes successful sounds while others do not.

In addition, the team hopes to understand why some populations of sage-grouse in the wilds of Wyoming are declining. Their work takes them into the field to study the courtship of these birds in nature. Patricelli and her colleagues suspect that noise pollution from nearby developments may be interfering with the female sage-grouse's ability to hear males during

Researcher Gail Patricelli of the University of California poses with the prototype of the robotic female sage-grouse, called a fembot.

A male sage-grouse (*background*) makes a courtship display while look-ing at the robotic female sage-grouse.

courtship. Patricelli's team hopes that the noise pollution research will help sage-grouse courtship and development to coexist in Wyoming. Noise, Patricelli points out, is possible to control.

As a graduate student trained in animal behavior and ecology, Patricelli studied the courtship behaviors of satin bowerbirds at the University of Maryland, College Park. She is currently an ecologist at the University of California, Davis in the Section of Evolution and Ecology.

MAMMAL COURTSHIP RESEARCHER: HEIDI FISHER

Heidi Fisher studied how the rare pygmy loris, a primate that fits easily in the palm of a human hand, uses its sense of smell

Scientists have observed that female pygmy lorises prefer counter-marking males.

during courtship. Fisher studied pygmy lorises living in captivity at a zoo.

Both male and female pygmy lorises use urine to mark their home ranges and communicate. Male pygmy lorises urinate, or mark, near where a female travels. One male will mark with urine, and another male will countermark near the first mark. The two males use these scent marks to compete for the attention of the female pygmy loris.

To understand countermarking, Fisher experimented with 19 captive lorises living behind the scenes at the San Diego Zoo when she was pursuing her master's degree at the University of California, San Diego.

In one experiment, Fisher collected urine samples from males and exposed them to other males. She was testing to see when and where the males would countermark. She found that some males tended to be countermarkers, meaning that they would urinate over an existing scent. Other males tended to be countermarked. In other words, they were the ones that had their scent marks challenged by other males.

Fisher then exposed individual female lorises to one male from each group. The females strongly preferred the counter-marking male—the one that would urinate over an existing scent. From this research, Fisher suggests that females prefer males that are better able to compete and saturate an area with their scent marks.

Today, Fisher is a researcher at Harvard University's Museum of Comparative Zoology. She continues to study animal courtship, and is currently working with deer mice to understand how sperm compete after mating is complete.

MORE RESEARCH TO COME

Understanding animal courtship—why animals behave the way they do when courting and mating—is an active field of animal behavior research. Researchers have already learned so much, but there is still much to be learned.

Glossary

Actinopterygians   All fish with fins and bones

Arachnid   Animals with jointed body parts, a hard outer shell (exoskeleton), no wings and no antennae

Arranged marriage   A marriage that is planned by people other than the individuals in the couple

Arthropod   An animal with a segmented body and a hard outer shell (exoskeleton). Spiders, insects, crustaceans, centipedes and scorpions are all arthropods.

Beetle   A type of insect with two pairs of wings. A pair of hard wings in front protects a pair of soft flying wings that are folded underneath.

Behavior   The response of an organism to signals or individuals in its environment

Bivalves   Mollusks with two-part shells, such as clams and oysters

Cephalopod   A type of mollusk. Many cephalopods have lost the mollusk shell, or it has become an internal shell. Octopuses, squids, cuttlefish and nautilus are all cephalopods.

Courtly love   The combination of a physical and very emotional desire for another person

Courtship   The process that results in two mature members of a species becoming a couple, usually with the intent to mate and produce offspring

Crustaceans   Animals with hard outer shells, antennae, and three body parts. Crabs, lobster, and shrimp are crustaceans.

Cuckolding Passing off parenting duties to another animal, without that animal knowing it

Diversity A measure of how many different types of things exist

Echinoderms Animals with spiny or rigid outside skins. Sea stars and sea urchins are echinoderms.

Ectotherms Cold-blooded animals

Evolution Change over time in the type and frequency of physical traits and behaviors in a population of organisms

Gestation The amount of time that a female mammal carries young in her body before they are born

Hermaphrodite A living thing that is both male and female at the same time

Intelligent design Contends that natural selection and evolution cannot be the only forces that shape life on Earth. The idea is that life is so "clever" that it must have an intelligent designer.

Introduced animals Animals that do not naturally live in an area, but have been moved there by humans, either on purpose or accidentally

Mating plug A barrier that prevents other males from mating with a female

Monogamous Mating with the same partner each breeding season

Native animals Animals that naturally live in an area

Natural history The study of plants and animals in their natural environments

Natural selection The process by which favorable characteristics and behaviors become more common in a population over time, and unfavorable characteristics and behaviors become less common or disappear

Pectines   Specialized organs on the underside of a scorpion that are used for touch

Pedipalps   A male spider's special set of arm-like appendages that hold and dispense sperm into a female during mating

Physical characteristic   An observable body part, such as a feather, fin, or antler, or a color or size

Salmonella   A disease naturally carried by reptiles that is potentially dangerous to humans

Sexual cannibalism   When one animal eats another during courtship or mating

Sexual conflict   When males and females have different goals during courtship and mating

Sexual dimorphism   When males and females of the same type of animal are different sizes or have different colors or body parts, such as antlers

Sexual selection   The idea that behaviors or physical characteristics that increase an animal's success during courtship and mating will spread through a population over time

Spawning   The process of releasing eggs into the water to mix with sperm and grow into new animals

Temperature-dependent sex determination   When the temperature of the eggs in a nest determines whether those eggs hatch as males or females

Ungulates   Hoofed mammals

Bibliography

Adler, Jerry, Anne Underwood, and William Lee Adams. "Charles Darwin: Evolution of a Scientist." *Newsweek* Vol. 146, Issue 22 (November 28, 2005).

Bell, Michael A. and Susan Adlai Foster. "The Evolutionary Biology of the Threespine Stickleback." Oxford University Press. (1994) 313-318.

Berreby, David. "Evolving by Accident, Not Fitness." *New York Times*. (October 14, 2003) University of Texas Web site. Available online. URL: http://www.sbs.utexas.edu/ryan/People.htm.

Dawkins, Richard. "The Illusion of Design." *Natural History Magazine* Web site. Available online. URL: http://www. naturalhistorymag.com/master.html?http://www.naturalhistory mag.com/1105/1105_feature1.html.

Dean, Cornelia. "In Lobster Courtship, Traits Like Humans." August 9, 2005. *New York Times* Web site. Available online. URL: http://www.nytimes.com/2005/08/09/science/09love.html.

Fiore, Andrew T. "Romantic Regressions: An Analysis of Behavior in Online Dating Systems." UC Berkeley Web site. Available online. URL: http://people.ischool.berkeley.edu/~atf/thesis_mit/.

Fisher, Heidi S. and G. G. Rosenthal. "Male swordtails court with an audience in mind." *Biology Letters*. (2007) 3: 5-7.

Fisher, Heidi S., R.R. Swaisgood, and H. Fitch-Snyder. "Counter-marking by male pygmy lorises (*Nycticebus pygmaeus*): Do females use odor cues to select mates with high competitive ability?" *Behavioral Ecology and Sociobiology*. (2003) 53: 123-130.

Fisher, Helen E. "The Biology of Attraction." *Psychology Today* Web site. Available online. URL: http://psychologytoday.com/articles/index.php?term=pto-19930301-000030&print=1.

Foote, C. J., G. S. Brown, and C.W. Hawryshyn. "Female colour and male choice in sockeye salmon: implications for the phenotypic convergence of anadromous and nonanadromous morphs." *Animal Behaviour.* (2004) 67: 69-83. CAB Abstracts Web site. Available online. URL: http://www.cababstractsplus.org/google/abstract.asp?AcNo=20043030640.

Gordon, David George. "The Complete Cockroach: A Comprehensive Guide to the Most Despised." Ten Speed Press. (1996) 65-69. Available online. URL: http://books.google.com/books?id=kk14saK7i5AC.

Goudarzi, Sara. "Birds Cut Rivals Off in Mating Songs." August 4, 2006. *LiveScience* Web site. Available online. URL: http://www.livescience.com/animals/060804_song_overlap.html.

Hany, Brian and Denise Pope. "Evidence of sexual conflict in the fiddler crab *Uca princeps.*" Submitted to *Proceedings of the Royal Society Biological Sciences.* Obtained by personal communication with Pope.

The Human Society of the United States. "Live Reptile Trade." The Humane Society Web site. Available online. URL: http://www.hsus.org/wildlife/issues_facing_wildlife/wildlife_trade/live_reptile_trade/.

Kendall, David. "Scorpions." Kendall Bioresearch Services Web site. Available online. URL: http://www.kendall-bioresearch.co.uk/scorpion.htm.

Lewis, Sara. "Summer flings: firefly courtship, sex, and death." Natural History. July-August 2003. FindArticles.com Web site. Available online. URL: http://findarticles.com/p/articles/mi_m1134/is_6_112/ai_105371466.

Losin, Neil. "King of the Western Sage." *Living Bird.* (Summer 2007) 10-19.

Macías Garcia, C. and E. Ramirez. "Evidence that sensory traps can evolve into honest signals." *Nature* 434 (2005) 501-505.

Madden, Mary and Amanda Lenhart. "Online Dating." The Pew Internet & American Life Project Web Site. Available online. URL: http://www.pewinternet.org/PPF/r/177/report_display.asp.

Myers, P. "Animal Diversity Web." University of Michigan Museum of Zoology. Available online. URL: http://animaldiversity. ummz.umich.edu/site/accounts/information/Animalia.html.

Phillips, Kathryn. "School Riddles; Schooling Fish." *International Wildlife*. National Wildlife Federation. Available online. URL: http://find articles.com/p/articles/mi_m1170/is_n2_v25/ai_16678894/print.

Pycraft, W.P. *The Courtship of Animals*. Whitefish, Montana: Kessinger Publishing, 2007.

ScienceDaily. "Role Reversal: Male Gets Easy Ride In Insect Courtship." *ScienceDaily* Web site. Available online. URL: http://www. sciencedaily.com/releases/2003/07/030725080035.htm.

Snow, LSE and Andrade, MCB. "Pattern of sperm transfer in redback spiders: Implications for sperm competition and male sacrifice." *Behavioral Ecology* 15(5) (2004) 785-792. Available online. URL: http://www.utsc.utoronto.ca/~mandrade/pdf/Snow_ Andrade2004.pdf?ijkey=10yMMM0B4nWjM&keytype=ref.

Stout, Prentice K. "Fish Schooling" Rhode Island Sea Grant Web site. Available online. URL: http://seagrant.gso.uri.edu/ factsheets/schooling.html.

Sulloway, Frank J. "The Evolution of Charles Darwin." *Smithsonian* Vol. 36, Issue 9 (December 2005): 58-69.

Wilson, Edward O. *The Diversity of Life*. New York: W. W. Norton & Company, 1999.

Zimmer, Carl. "This Can't be Love." New York Times Web site. Available online. URL: http://www.nytimes.com/2006/ 09/05/science/05cann.html?_r=4&oref=slogin&oref=slogin&oref =slogin&oref=slogin.

Further Resources

Ackerman, Diane. *The Rarest of the Rare*. New York: Random House, 1995.

Bradley, James V. *How Species Change*. New York: Chelsea House, 2006.

Givens, David. *Love Signals: A Practical Field Guide to the Body Language of Courtship*. New York: St. Martin's Press, 2004.

Hare, Tony. *Animal Life Cycles: Growing Up in the Wild*. New York: Facts On File Natural Science Library, 2001.

Hickman, Pamela. *Animals and Their Mates: How Animals Attract, Fight for and Protect Each Other*. Tonawanda, NY: Kids Can Press, 2004.

Hoose, Phillip. *The Race to Save the Lord God Bird*. New York: Farrar, Straus and Giroux, 2004.

Johnson, Vargie. *Charles Darwin, The Discoverer*. Chattaroy, WA: Kiwe Publishing, 2006.

Kirschner, Marc W. and John C. Gerhart. *The Plausibility of Life: Resolving Darwin's Dilemma*. New Haven, CT: Yale University Press, 2005.

Sloan, Christopher, M. Leakey, and L. Leakey. *The Human Story: Our Evolution from Prehistoric Ancestors to Today*. Washington, D.C.: National Geographic Children's Books, 2004.

Strauss, Rochelle. *Tree of Life: The Incredible Biodiversity of Life on Earth*. Tonawanda, NY: Kids Can Press, 2004.

Walker, Sally. *Crocodiles*. Minneapolis: Learner Publications, 2004.

WEB SITES

"BioKids"
University of Michigan
http://www.biokids.umich.edu/
Includes a "Critter Catalog" focused on the diversity of animals.

Science News for Kids
http://www.sciencenewsforkids.org/
Search for the latest news on animal courtship research here.

"Understanding Evolution"
University of California Museum of Paleontology
National Center for Science Education
http://evolution.berkeley.edu/evolibrary/home.php
The basics of evolution, including Darwin's theory of natural selection, for young people.

The Whalesong Project
http://www.whalesong.net/
Listen and learn about whale songs online.

"Wildfinder: Mapping the World's Species"
World Wildlife Fund
http://www.worldwildlife.org/wildfinder/
Search for a species and see where it lives.

Picture Credits

Index

115

About the Author

Krista West always has been interested in educating people about the behavior of animals. She majored in zoology at the University of Washington, later volunteering at the New England Aquarium and the Bronx Zoo. After earning master's degrees in Journalism and Earth Science, both from Columbia University in New York, West has spent more than 10 years writing about science topics. She lives in Fairbanks, Alaska, with her husband and two sons and is a firm believer in love at first sight.